Best Friends Bakery

Clean & Natural Dog Treat Recipes

Vivian Codiga

Best Friends Bakery

© 2017 Vivian Codiga

Published By: Austin Startup School
AustinStartUpSchool.com
ISBN: 0-9990182-2-1
ISBN-13: 978-0-9990182-2-4

Dedication

This book is dedicated to my parents for guiding me through writing this book, and through life. It is also dedicated to the people (and canines!) around me who inspired me to write for them, and inspire me everyday to grow into a better version of myself.

Special thanks to Austin StartUp School for inviting me to unleash my creativity in a book and for guiding me through the process, from idea to implementation!

Contents

Introduction

Best Friends Bakery: Clean & Natural Dog Treat Recipes is a result of my commitment to improve the health and the lives of animals - and therefore, the lives of their owners!

I know all too well the discomfort and ill effects that irritating foods can have on a digestive system and on quality of life, in general. It's been a long process of exploration, trial, error and discovery to find a diet that has significantly reduced the inflammation that once ravaged my gut! I feel so relieved, and I want so much for my canine friends to feel relieved, too.

Imagine the harmony you'll feel with your dog when you can freely enjoy your lives together without the symptoms of an inflamed gut soiling your plans! Skin rashes, ear infections, messy potty problems and frequent vet visits will soon be replaced with healthy functioning body systems and a lifestyle unencumbered by illness. It's time to be free!

In the pages of this book you'll find 21 savory and sweet recipes for treats that are free from common allergens and inflammatory ingredients. Classified as gluten-free, grain-free and or/paleo, you can feel confident you are feeding your dog clean and natural treats that they'll love, and won't regret consuming later!

I promise that you and your dog will love these treats, and will no longer need to continue your search to find the perfect one. With over 20 treats below $8 with 8 ingredients or less, you're sure to find the perfect one (or more!) here.

Happy baking!

Best Friends Bakery

Savory

peanut butter & pumpkin

paleo, gluten-free, grain-free

Time: 25 mins

Quantity: 50 treats

- 1 1/2 cup coconut flour
- 1/2 cup peanut butter - no added ingredients
- 3 eggs
- 1/2 cup coconut oil
- 1 cup + 2 Tbsp pumpkin puree

1. Preheat oven to 350 degrees
2. Combine all ingredients in a mixing bowl and form the dough into a ball
3. Between two sheets of parchment paper, roll out the dough to approximately ¼ inch
4. Use your desired cookie cutters and gently press them into the dough
5. Transfer them to a parchment lined baking sheet and bake for 12-15 minutes
6. Let cool completely before serving

Best Friends Bakery

bacon & cheddar

gluten-free

Time: 20 mins

Quantity: 25 treats

- 4 strips bacon, cooked crisply and chopped finely

- 1/3 cup shredded cheddar cheese

- 1 1/2 cup cooked oatmeal (rolled oats)

- 2 eggs

1. Preheat oven to 350 degrees

2. Combine bacon, cheese, and oatmeal in mixing bowl.

3. Add eggs to the dry mixture to form a thick sticky dough

4. Roll dough out to approximately 1/4 of an inch. Use cookie cutters to cut out desired shapes

5. Bake treats on a parchment paper lined baking tray for approximately 20 minutes

6. Let cool completely before serving

Best Friends Bakery

turkey & sweet potato

paleo, gluten-free, grain-free

Time: 40 mins

Quantity: 50 treats

- 1 1/2 cup coconut flour

- 1/2 cup peanut butter - no added ingredients

- 4 eggs

- 1/2 cup coconut oil

- 1/2 cup diced plain turkey meat, diced finely

- 1 cup sweet potato or pumpkin puree

1. Preheat oven to 350 degrees

2. Combine all ingredients in a mixing bowl and form the dough into a ball

3. Between two sheets of parchment paper, roll out the dough to approximately ¼ inch

4. Use your desired cookie cutters and gently press them into the dough

5. Transfer to a parchment lined baking sheet and bake for 12-15 minutes

6. Let cool completely before serving

Best Friends Bakery

parmesan & potato

paleo, gluten-free, grain-free

Time: 40 mins

Quantity: 50 treats

- 1 1/2 cup coconut flour
- 1/2 cup peanut butter, no added ingredients
- 3 eggs
- 1/2 cup coconut oil
- 1/4 cup grated parmesan cheese
- 3/4 cup mashed potatoes, no added ingredients

1. Preheat oven to 350 degrees
2. Combine all ingredients in a mixing bowl and form the dough into a ball. If too dry, add another egg.
3. Between two sheets of parchment paper, roll out the dough to approximately ¼ inch
4. Use your desired cookie cutters and gently press them into the dough
5. Transfer to a parchment lined baking sheet and bake for 12-15 minutes
6. Let cool completely before serving

Best Friends Bakery

spinach & carrot

paleo, gluten-free, grain-free

Time: 25 mins

Quantity: 50 treats

- 1 1/2 cup coconut flour

- 1/2 cup peanut butter - no added ingredients

- 4 eggs

- 1/2 cup coconut oil

- 1/2 cup finely chopped spinach

- 1/2 cup shredded carrots

1. Preheat oven to 350 degrees

2. Combine all ingredients in a mixing bowl and form the dough into a ball

3. Between two sheets of parchment paper, roll out the dough to approximately ¼ inch

4. Use your desired cookie cutters and gently press them into the dough

5. Transfer to a parchment lined baking sheet and bake for 12-15 minutes

6. Let cool completely before serving

Best Friends Bakery

peanut butter & bacon

paleo, gluten-free, grain-free

Time: 25 mins

Quantity: 50 treats

- 1/2 cup coconut flour
- 3/4 cup peanut butter - no added ingredients
- 4 eggs
- 1/2 cup coconut oil
- 3/4 cup finely diced bacon

1. Preheat oven to 350 degrees
2. Combine all ingredients in a mixing bowl and form the dough into a ball
3. Between two sheets of parchment paper, roll out the dough to approximately ¼ inch
4. Use your desired cookie cutters and gently press them into the dough
5. Transfer to a parchment lined baking sheet and bake for 12-15 minutes
6. Let cool completely before serving.

Best Friends Bakery

quinoa & sweet potato

paleo, gluten-free, grain-free

Time: 55 mins

Quantity: 50 treats

- 1/2 cup coconut flour

- 1/2 cup peanut butter - no added ingredients

- 4 eggs

- 1/2 cup coconut oil

- 1/2 cup cooked quinoa

- 1/2 cup sweet potato puree

1. Preheat oven to 350 degrees

2. Combine all ingredients in a mixing bowl and form the dough into a ball

3. Between two sheets of parchment paper, roll out the dough to approximately ¼ inch

4. Use your desired cookie cutters and gently press them into the dough

5. Transfer to a parchment lined baking sheet and bake for 12-15 minutes

6. Let cool completely before serving

Best Friends Bakery

Sweet

blueberry & banana

paleo, gluten-free, grain-free

Time: 30 mins

Quantity: 35 treats

- **1 cup coconut flour**

- **1/2 cup of peanut butter - no added ingredients**

- **1/2 cup of mashed blueberries**

- **1/2 cup of mashed bananas**

- **3 eggs**

- **1/3 cup of warm water**

1. Preheat your oven to 350 degrees

2. In a large bowl, combine all ingredients and mix thoroughly. Add another egg if too dry.

3. Roll out dough to approximately ¼ inch and cut out desired shapes

4. Transfer them to a parchment lined baking sheet

5. Bake in the oven for 22 minutes

6. Let cool completely before serving

Best Friends Bakery

frozen strawberry & banana smoothie

paleo, gluten-free, grain-free

Time: 4 hours or more

Quantity: 30 treats

- 2 cups sliced strawberries or a 16 ounce bag of frozen strawberries

- 1 1/2 cups Plain Low Fat Yogurt

- 1 banana

- 1/4 cup of coconut milk

- 3 tablespoons of honey

1. Place all the ingredients in your blender

2. Turn on the blender to a medium speed (or smoothie setting)

3. Pour into the molds of your choice or use ice cube trays

4. Freeze for 4 hours or more

5. Pop out of the molds

6. Ready to ENJOY!

Best Friends Bakery

frozen watermelon & mint

paleo, gluten-free, grain-free

Time: 4 hours or more

Quantity: 30 treats

- 2 cups chopped watermelon

- 1 1/2 cups plain low fat yogurt

- 2 tablespoons chopped mint

- 1/4 cup of coconut milk

- 3 tablespoons of honey

7. Place all the ingredients in your blender

8. Turn on the blender to a medium speed (or smoothie setting)

9. Pour into the molds of your choice or use ice cube trays

10. Freeze for 4 hours or more

11. Pop out of the molds

12. Ready to ENJOY!

coconut & cranberry

paleo, gluten-free, grain-free

Time: 25 mins

Quantity: 50 treats

- 1 1/2 cup coconut flour

- 1/2 cup peanut butter - no added ingredients

- 4 eggs

- 1/2 cup coconut oil

- 1/2 cup dried cranberries (no sugar added)

- 1/4 cup dried coconut flakes (unsweetened)

1. Preheat oven to 350 degrees

2. Combine all ingredients in a mixing bowl and form the dough into a ball

3. Between two sheets of parchment paper, roll out the dough to approximately ¼ inch

4. Use your desired cookie cutters and gently press them into the dough

5. Transfer to a parchment lined baking sheet and bake for 12-15 minutes

6. Let cool completely before serving

Best Friends Bakery

honey & sweet potato

paleo, gluten-free, grain-free

Time: 40 mins

Quantity: 50 treats

- 1 1/2 cup coconut flour

- 1/2 cup peanut butter - no added ingredients

- 3 eggs

- 1/2 cup coconut oil

- 1/3 cup honey

- 2/3 cup mashed sweet potatoes - no added ingredients

1. Preheat oven to 350 degrees

2. Combine all ingredients in a mixing bowl and form the dough into a ball

3. Between two sheets of parchment paper, roll out the dough to approximately ¼ inch

4. Use your desired cookie cutters and gently press them into the dough

5. Transfer to a parchment lined baking sheet and bake for 12-15 minutes

6. Let cool completely before serving

Best Friends Bakery

carob & strawberry

paleo, gluten-free, grain-free

Time: 25 mins

Quantity: 50 treats

- 1 1/2 cup coconut flour
- 1/2 cup peanut butter - no added ingredients
- 4 eggs
- 1/2 cup coconut oil
- 1/4 cup carob powder
- 3/4 cup diced strawberries

1. Preheat oven to 350 degrees
2. Combine all ingredients in a mixing bowl and form the dough into a ball
3. Between two sheets of parchment paper, roll out the dough to approximately ¼ inch
4. Use your desired cookie cutters and gently press them into the dough
5. Transfer to a parchment lined baking sheet and bake for 12-15 minutes
6. Let cool completely before serving

Best Friends Bakery

apple & honey

paleo, gluten-free, grain-free

Time: 25 mins

Quantity: 50 treats

- 1 1/2 cup coconut flour

- 1/2 cup peanut butter - no added ingredients

- 3 eggs

- 1/2 cup coconut oil

- 2/3 cup finely diced apples

- 1/3 cup honey

1. Preheat oven to 350 degrees

2. Combine all ingredients in a mixing bowl and form the dough into a ball

3. Between two sheets of parchment paper, roll out the dough to approximately ¼ inch

4. Use your desired cookie cutters and gently press them into the dough

5. Transfer to a parchment lined baking sheet and bake for 12-15 minutes

6. Let cool completely before serving

Best Friends Bakery

Sweet & Savory

chicken & apple

paleo, gluten-free, grain-free

Time: 25 mins

Quantity: 50 treats

- 1/2 cup coconut flour
- 1/2 cup peanut butter - no added ingredients
- 4 organic eggs
- 1/2 cup coconut oil
- 1/2 cup finely diced plain chicken meat
- 1/2 cup finely diced apple slices

1. Preheat oven to 350 degrees
2. Combine all ingredients in a mixing bowl and form the dough into a ball
3. Between two sheets of parchment paper, roll out the dough to approximately ¼ inch
4. Use your desired cookie cutters and gently press them into the dough
5. Transfer to a parchment lined baking sheet and bake for 12-15 minutes
6. Let cool completely before serving

Best Friends Bakery

carob & peanut butter

paleo, gluten-free, grain-free

Time: 25 mins

Quantity: 50 treats

- 1 1/2 cup coconut flour

- 3/4 cup peanut butter - no added ingredients

- 4 eggs

- 1/2 cup coconut oil

- 1/2 cup carob powder

1. Preheat oven to 350 degrees

2. Combine all ingredients in a mixing bowl and form the dough into a ball

3. Between two sheets of parchment paper, roll out the dough to approximately ¼ inch

4. Use your desired cookie cutters and gently press them into the dough

5. Transfer to a parchment lined baking sheet and bake for 12-15 minutes

6. Let cool completely before serving

Best Friends Bakery

peanut butter & banana

paleo, gluten-free, grain-free

Time: 25

Quantity: 50 treats

- 1 1/2 cup coconut flour

- 1 cup peanut butter - no added ingredients

- 3 eggs

- 1/2 cup coconut oil

- 2 ripe bananas, mashed

1. Preheat oven to 350 degrees

2. Combine all ingredients in a mixing bowl and form the dough into a ball

3. Between two sheets of parchment paper, roll out the dough to approximately ¼ inch

4. Use your desired cookie cutters and gently press them into the dough

5. Transfer to a parchment lined baking sheet and bake for 12-15 minutes

6. Let cool completely before serving

Best Friends Bakery

chicken & apricot

paleo, gluten-free, grain-free

Time: 25 mins

Quantity: 50 treats

- 1 1/2 cup coconut flour

- 1/2 cup peanut butter - no added ingredients

- 4 eggs

- 1/2 cup coconut oil

- 1/2 cup finely diced plain chicken

- 1/2 cup finely diced dried apricots

1. Preheat oven to 350 degrees.

2. Combine all ingredients in a mixing bowl and form the dough into a ball

3. Between two sheets of parchment paper, roll out the dough to approximately ¼ inch

4. Use your desired cookie cutters and gently press them into the dough

5. Transfer to a parchment lined baking sheet and bake for 12-15 minutes

6. Let cool completely before serving

Best Friends Bakery

mango & chicken

paleo, gluten-free, grain-free

Time: 25 mins

Quantity: 50 treats

- 1 1/2 cup coconut flour

- 1/2 cup peanut butter - no added ingredients

- 4 eggs

- 1/2 cup coconut oil

- 1/2 cup finely diced mango

- 1/2 cup finely diced plain chicken

1. Preheat oven to 350 degrees

2. Combine all ingredients in a mixing bowl and form the dough into a ball.

3. Between two sheets of parchment paper, roll out the dough to approximately ¼ inch

4. Use your desired cookie cutters and gently press them into the dough

5. Transfer to a parchment lined baking sheet and bake for 12-15 minutes

6. Let cool completely before serving

Best Friends Bakery

honey & carrot

paleo, gluten-free, grain-free

Time: 25 mins

Quantity: 50 treats

- 1 1/2 cup coconut flour

- 1/2 cup peanut butter - no added ingredients

- 3 eggs

- 1/2 cup coconut oil

- 1/3 cup honey

- 2/3 cup finely shredded carrots

1. Preheat oven to 350 degrees

2. Combine all ingredients in a mixing bowl and form the dough into a ball. If too dry, add another egg.

3. Between two sheets of parchment paper, roll out the dough to approximately ¼ inch

4. Use your desired cookie cutters and gently press them into the dough

5. Transfer to a parchment lined baking sheet and bake for 12-15 minutes

6. Let cool completely before serving

Best Friends Bakery

maple & bacon

paleo, gluten-free, grain-free

Time: 25 mins

Quantity: 50 treats

- 1 1/2 cup coconut flour

- 1/2 cup peanut butter

- 4 eggs

- 1/2 cup coconut oil

- 1/3 cup maple syrup

- 2/3 cup finely diced bacon

1. Preheat oven to 350 degrees

2. Combine all ingredients in a mixing bowl and form the dough into a ball.

3. Between two sheets of parchment paper, roll out the dough to approximately ¼ inch

4. Use your desired cookie cutters and gently press them into the dough

5. Transfer to a parchment lined baking sheet and bake for 12-15 minutes

6. Let cool completely before serving

Best Friends Bakery

Did You Know?

Some common household foods can be very harmful for your pet.
Here are some of the common culprits that may result in a trip to the vet!
Are you feeding your dog anything on this list?
Please do your own research and check with your vet about foods your dog should avoid.

Food	Side Effects
Cinnamon	diarrhea, vomiting, increased or decreased heart rate, and liver disease
Garlic, Onions, Leeks, and Chives	pale gums, elevated heart rate, weakness, and collapsing
Macadamia Nuts	vomiting, increased body temperature, inability to walk, lethargy
Xylitol	vomiting, lethargy, coordination problems, seizures, and liver failure
Fat Trimmings and Bones	pancreatitis
Chocolate	diarrhea, vomiting, seizures, and irregular heart function
Avocado	vomiting and diarrhea
Cherries	dilated pupils, difficulty breathing, and red gums
Salt	nausea, respiratory distress, seizures, stomach pains, and tongue swelling
Grapes	sudden kidney failure

Source: American Kennel Club http://www.akc.org/

About Me

Hi, I'm Vivian Codiga, an aspiring actress and animal lover.

I love baking, hanging out with friends, going to the beach, acting, and being around little kids. When I'm not researching , writing and testing recipes, you can find me in theatre class, at triathlon training or deep in the wilderness learning primitive skills!

I love a challenge and in true form, I gladly accepted the invitation from my parents to unleash my voice in a book. I'm always looking for new and creative ways to express myself, so writing a book blending two of my favorite things was a no-brainer!

I look forward to the next challenge. Got any ideas?

You can email me at: authorviviancodiga@gmail.com

Please also consider leaving me a review on Amazon.com.

Your review helps this book reach more dogs and their owners and change more lives.

Best Friends Bakery

Made in the USA
Lexington, KY
17 April 2019